Jay Cooper

the SPY NEXT DOOR

Mutant Rat Attack!

SCHOLASTIC PRESS
NEW YORK

For Mom, who was never too busy on a Saturday to laugh along with me at *The Giant Claw*, or cry with me over *Mighty Joe Young*.

Library of Congress Cataloging-in-Publication Data

ISBN 978-93-86313-93-5

10 9 8 7 6 5 4 3 2 1 17 18 19 20 21

First edition, January 2017

Book design by Nina Goffi

Reprinted by Scholastic India Pvt. Ltd., August 2017

Printed at Batra Art Press, New Delhi - 28

CHAPTER 1

Daring Dreams and Mad Dashes!

It looked like the end of the road for Dexter Drabner, Secret Spy.

Here he was, trapped in the lair of the massively evil Commandant Cranium, facing certain doom. Tied tightly to his own skateboard with metal coils, he rolled slowly down a conveyor belt toward the Death Dicer, a swinging globe covered in blades that would chop him up into bite-size Dexter Drabner bits. To make matters worse, the top secret information on the flash drive that Dexter had been assigned to retrieve was now in the hands of the mad scientist with the glass-encased brain.

"So the world-famous Secret Spy is finally in my clutches!" Commandant Cranium cackled. "Ogor, turn the conveyor-belt speed from **SLOW** to **MEDIUM**, and then turn the spikes on the Death Dicer from **SHARP** to **REALLY, REALLY SHARP!** Mwah-ha-ha-ha!"

MWAH-
HA-HA-HA!
hee hee!
PUSH!
—OMG!
—Fast
—Medium
—Slow

The drive!
Mein brain!

"Not so fast, Commandant Cranium!" cried Dexter. He suddenly threw the metal coils over the side of the conveyor belt and leapt up onto his skateboard. He triumphantly held up a bent paper clip.

Cranium's glass-encased brain pulsated with anger. "The swine has freed himself from my coils with only a paper clip!"

Dexter shot down the conveyor belt atop the skateboard toward the Death Dicer, ollied over the railing, and in one swift motion, snatched the flash drive out of Cranium's hands and gave him a good-bye kick.

Commandant Cranium shrieked in pain. His cry sounded a lot like an alarm clock going off.

All at once, the laboratory scene dissolved. The lair's giant electrodes transformed into Dexter's bedposts, and the dangerous Death Dicer turned into Dexter's ceiling fan. Dexter Drabner blinked. He slowly realized that he had been dreaming.

For a moment, disappointment flooded him. Back to boring old real life . . .

Then, suddenly, Dexter's eyes popped wide open as he remembered something even more important than a death-defying dream: his **ESSAY**! He'd stayed up late for an important homework assignment, and had trudged sleepily off to bed before completing it. He ran to his desk and scrambled to finish the report.

The essay was a no-brainer for Dex. The topic was "What Is Your Dream Job?" He had chosen to write about his hero, Toby Falcon, world-famous professional skateboarder and hero of the Skate Spy movies. What better job in this world could there be than being paid to skateboard, star in movies as a superspy, and be the idol of millions of adoring fans?

He finished the essay and reread it quickly. "Well, it's not exactly Shakespeare, but it'll have to do," Dexter said to himself, and hastily signed his name.

TOBY FALCON!

He dressed as quickly as he could, grabbed his book bag, and dashed through the front door. He flew down the apartment building steps like a rocket. Dexter's school was only a few short blocks away from where his family lived in Girder City, but he was super late. He didn't even have time to stuff his essay into his bag. He just gripped the pages tightly in one hand as his sneakers slapped the pavement in his mad sprint to the school.

HO-HUM HERALD
BORING SINCE 1922
BROCCOLI STOLEN FROM LAB!
YAWN
WORLD'S GREATEST ACCOUNTANT

He was just rounding the corner of the avenue to the school when tragedy struck.

Literally.

One minute hope filled Dexter's eyes as he noted a few other stragglers still hustling to school ahead of him. The next minute he was flying head over heels, the pages of his essay scattering everywhere!

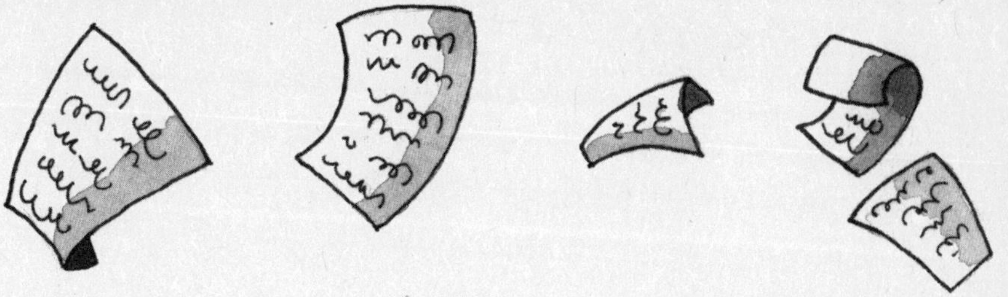

“**OOPS!**” bellowed a loud voice, brimming with nastiness. The voice belonged to Millicent, Dexter’s next-door neighbor—and more importantly, the biggest bully on the block. It was obvious from the smirk on her face that she’d purposely sent Dexter sprawling.

“My essay!” Dexter cried as the pages were carried off by the breeze.

“AW, GEEZ! DID I DO THAT? GUESS I DIDN’T SEE YOU THERE, BLAND BOY!”

A List of Millicent's Boring

Dexter grimaced at the name. Millicent was always coming up with new and terrible nicknames for Dexter. She thought he was impossibly boring and teased him about it every chance she got. The worst part was, Dexter believed her. His life was boring. His clothes were boring. His parents were especially boring. He didn't even have a pet. Well, he'd had a goldfish once, but it had died . . . probably of boredom.

Names for Dexter Drabner!

But he didn't have time to focus on any of that now. All he could do was chase the pages of his essay, which flew in the hot city wind.

Millicent cried after him, **"SORRY ABOUT THAT, DRABNER! GOOD LUCK GETTING TO SCHOOL ON TIME, LAME-O! HAR HAR!"**

Dexter scooped up two of the pages, but the others were perilously close to the subway stairs. He lunged for them, but it was too late. With a look of horror, he watched as his homework flew into the darkness of the subway entrance.

Dexter grabbed one page as it came to rest on the bottom step. He pounced on another that had wrapped itself around a subway turnstile. Now there was only one last page to save. Dexter watched as it flitted past the turnstile onto the platform.

"Great. Just great," Dexter muttered under his breath.

He had no choice but to duck beneath the turnstile and go in after it.

He chased the page to the very edge of the subway platform, grabbing it as it threatened to go over the edge and down to the tunnel floor. He'd saved his homework! He looked up, and immediately forgot his victory as he noticed what was right in front of him.

Pasted to the subway wall was a poster for the newest Skate Spy movie! **Skate Spy 6: Attack of the Android Ninjas!** It looked . . .

SKATE SPY6
in Attack of the Android Ninjas!
Action!
Adventure!
More Action!
No Romance!

"Listen, if you're not gonna tip, can you at least take your sneaker outta my hat?"

A girl with a guitar leaned against the tiled wall. She was older than Dexter, maybe old enough to be in the seventh grade. By far the strangest thing about her was the eye patch she wore. The patch did not look pleased.

"Holy guacamole!" Dexter said. "I didn't see you!"

The girl plucked a few strings of her guitar. “Are you a music fan? I take requests.”

She started to play the James Bond theme song, and not particularly well.

Her playing was so bad, Dexter winced. “Wow, that’s sure . . . music . . . but, uh, I’m really late for school.” He pulled out a quarter and tossed it into the hat. “Bye,” he said, and ran off down the platform.

The girl with the eye patch watched him go. “Sucker,” she muttered under her breath.

CHAPTER 2

Skate Rats and Mind Molders!

Dexter slunk into science class a half hour late.

He loved Mr. McFur's science class, but not because Mr. McFur was such a great teacher. It was the rats. Mr. McFur's classroom was covered in rats. Hundreds of them lined the walls in cages. Some slept. Some ate. Dozens ran on little squeaky exercise wheels.

"Running late today, Dexter?" asked Mr. McFur. But he didn't wait for an answer.

Mr. McFur had a familiar wild look in his eye. The class watched him in silence. All they could hear was the sound of hundreds of tiny rat farts. That's right—the passing of lots and lots of tiny puffs of gas. Call them toots if you prefer. They were part of . . .

LUCKY DRAGON
1.
MILK
SNAP!
LUCKY DRAGON
2.
MR. McFUR'S STINKTASTIC,
MILK 2½%
5.
6.

FARTERIFIC DISCOVERY!

Before Mr. McFur had hundreds of rats, he'd had just one. Her name was Pretty Princess Fabulous (Pretty for short). Pretty was smart—she could even do a few tricks. And she **LOVED** to eat.

Once, in the teachers' lounge, Pretty spotted a carton of Mr. McFur's leftover Chinese food—beef and broccoli—sitting unguarded on the lounge table. She couldn't resist.

By the time Mr. McFur returned from the refrigerator with his milk, Pretty had devoured the whole thing.

Mr. McFur started to chide her, but then Pretty let out the biggest toot in rat history—it was loud, startling, a little stinky, and **AMAZING**.

When Pretty farted, all the lights in the classroom flickered and then blew out.

Mr. McFur had discovered that rat gas contained electric power! Ever since, Mr. McFur had been attempting to duplicate that gassy power surge, but with no success.

Now Mr. McFur paced in front of the class.

“As you know,” he began, “rat gas is a huge untapped natural energy resource! If harnessed correctly, it will solve all the world’s energy problems.”

Everyone nodded, but no one in the class actually believed Mr. McFur’s kooky ideas.

“Pretty is an exceptional rat. She’ll eat anything put in front of her.” McFur patted Pretty appreciatively. “But these rodents . . .” He raised his hands to indicate the other rats around the room. “They refuse to eat the broccoli.

“And it’s broccoli that creates the megafarts necessary to prove my Rat Gas Power theorem. That has been the problem . . . until now!”

Mr. McFur held up a ring of rolled aluminum with a couple of random wires and two tiny radar dishes sticking out of it at opposite ends. “I worked all night on this, students. Can you guess what it is?”

Millicent raised her hand. “Is it the crown that will make you king of the **CUCKOOS**?”

“Ha-ha!” Mr. McFur sneered. “They laughed at me over at the patent office, too, when I tried to patent Rat Gas Power™. But soon they won’t be laughing anymore! This, class, is a Rat Mind Molder, also ™. Once I put this on, my little friends will do whatever I tell them.” He lowered the aluminum crown to his head.

Seven of the rats suddenly stood on their back legs, unlocked their cages, and climbed up onto Mr. McFur's desk in a line. Each held a little skateboard in its tiny paws. In unison they started zipping around Mr. McFur's desk.

The class began to clap. Mr. McFur clapped along with them. “Ha-ha! It’s working. As I always say, ‘You can give a rat a skateboard but you can’t make him skate . . . unless, of course, you have a Rat Mind Molder still TM!’”

The sound of someone clearing her throat interrupted the class celebration.

Principal Pickles stood in the doorway looking glum. “Mr. McFur, may I speak to you for a moment?”

Mr. McFur looked worried. “Yes, of course. Class, I’ll be right back.”

Dexter wondered what the problem could be. He watched Mr. McFur and Ms. Pickles closely through the glass window in the door, and saw his teacher begin to shake.

When Mr. McFur reentered the class, he was wiping his nose on his sleeve. He had obviously been crying.

"Class," he began sadly, "I've had some terrible news. Apparently, some p . . . p . . . parent c . . . c . . . complained that my rats are making learning difficult and the school board plans to confiscate them t . . . t . . . tomorrow."

Then he started crying uncontrollably, and the entire class rushed to console Mr. McFur. All except for one student. Millicent sat at her desk with an angelic smile on her face. But Dexter knew Millicent was no angel.

She must have been the one who complained about Mr. McFur's rats! thought Dexter. He was determined to do something about it.

CHAPTER 3

Unlikely Spies and Mysterious Strangers!

After school, Dexter snuck back to Mr. McFur's classroom. He headed over to Millicent's desk through a cloud of rat farts.

Dexter knew that Millicent rarely paid attention in class. She mostly just passed mean notes to her friends Francesca and Daisy. If he could find a note that made fun of Mr. McFur, or anything that might prove that Millicent was lying about the rats distracting her from learning, Dexter might be able to save his teacher's rats.

He opened the desktop slowly. Eureka! Dexter grabbed a folded piece of paper and held it up to the light. It read:

Oh, woe is me? Alas? Something was fishy.

And then it dawned on Dexter. Millicent knew it might get out that she'd made the complaint. She was planting evidence to frame Mr. McFur!

Suddenly Dexter heard voices outside the classroom. And then the doorknob turned.

Dexter had no time to look for a place to hide. He dove under Millicent's desk, closed his eyes, and hoped he would not be seen.

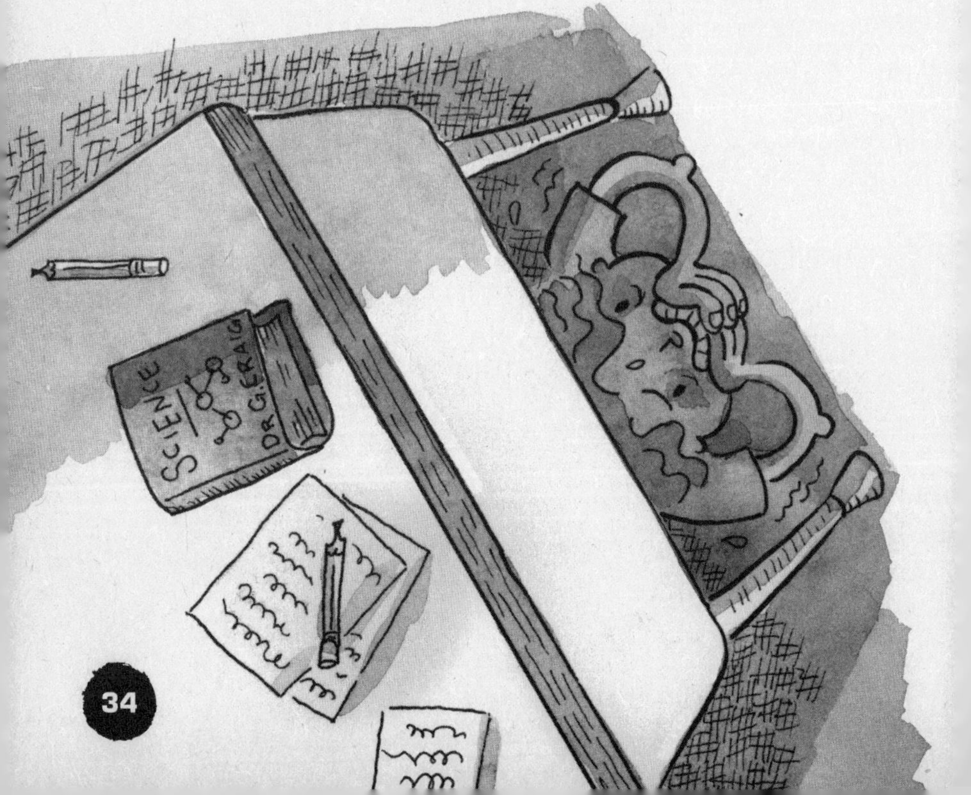

“Well, sir, I came as you r . . . r . . . requested. Sob!”

That’s Mr. McFur’s voice! thought Dexter. *That’s definitely Mr. McFur’s crying!*

“Yes. I’ve heard about your unfortunate rat situation. And I’m here to help!”

The second voice sounded oddly familiar. Dexter couldn’t place where he’d heard it before, but could tell it was really close. The two men were right in front of Millicent’s desk! Dexter held his breath.

The stranger continued. “I have heard about your rat gas theory. Furthermore, I think it will work!”

“You do? No one else does—besides me, of course,” said Mr. McFur sadly.

The stranger hissed, "You just need something to prove your genius to the masses! Once they see the amazing results of rat gas power for themselves, they'll let you keep your little . . . um . . . friends."

"But how???" cried Mr. McFur. "I have not been able to replicate my results from the teachers' lounge!"

"Maybe **THIS** will help!" the mysterious stranger replied gleefully.

Dexter heard rattling. Then Mr. McFur said, "Your car keys?"

"Oh, er, sorry. Wrong pocket. Let me just check . . . **YES!** I mean . . . **THIS!!!!!**"

Mr. McFur gasped. "Gamma broccoli! But that's radioactive. It's dangerous—and not at all legal!"

"Oh, legal shmegal," said the stranger. "What does it matter? If it works, you get to keep your precious rats. Here! Take it."

"Oh geez!" cried Mr. McFur. "Whoops! It's slipping!"

Something dropped in front of Dexter, but was plucked out of the air by thin, manicured fingers. It was a head of broccoli. And it was glowing!

"Good heavens, man!" growled the stranger. "Be careful! I'm going to place this on the desk, where your pudgy butterfingers won't blow up the whole school! Now, tomorrow, when Principal Pickles tries to take your precious pets, use the gamma broccoli and . . . KAPOW!"

Dex had heard all he could stand. Eyes squeezed tightly, he shot out from under the desk, zipped between the men's legs, and ran straight for the door!

Mr. McFur sputtered a strangled exclamation. "Hey! You shouldn't be in here!"

And from the stranger came a furious roar. "Get him!"

Dexter burst through the door and kept running.

Mr. McFur followed, sweating and puffing as he ran. McFur might have been four times Dexter's size, but he wasn't in great shape and Dexter was fast as lightning when he needed to be.

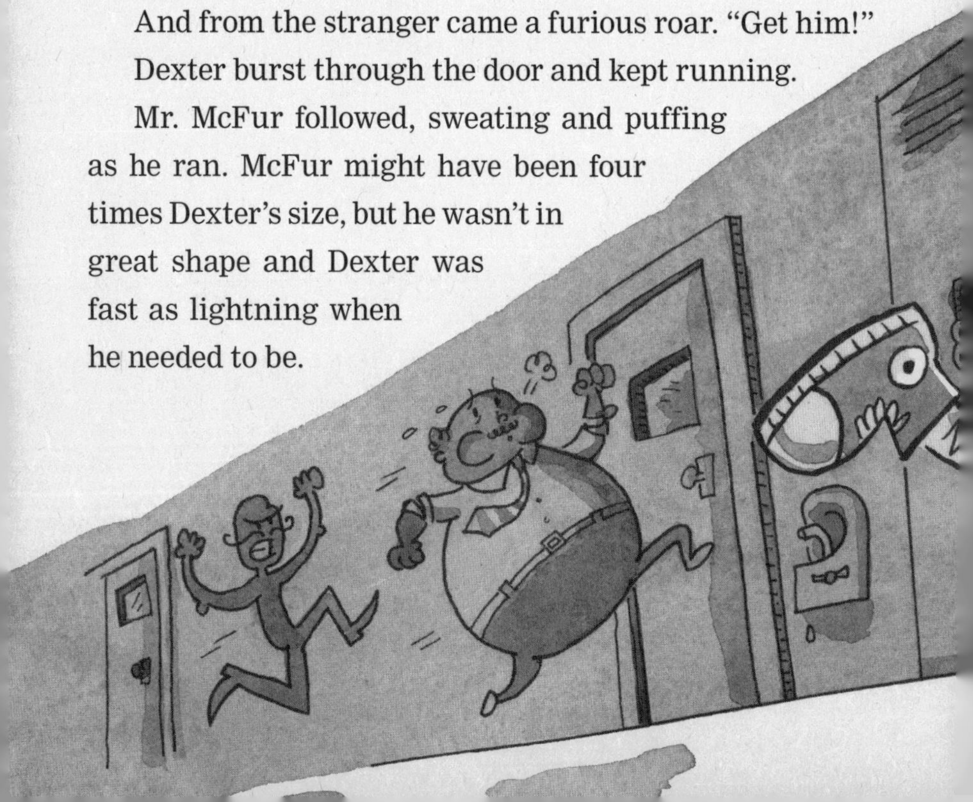

KIRBY RICHARDS
ELEMENTARY
Go Unicorns!!!!

Dexter turned down the hallway and quickly ducked into the main office. He looked around the darkened room. There was only one real hiding place in here: the Lost & Found closet, a place from which no toy or piece of clothing was ever heard from again. He opened the door. Inside the dark, shadowy room, Dexter spied an enormous mountain of discarded sweaters, jackets, Frisbees, and lunch boxes.

Just then, he heard voices right outside the office.

"I think he went this way!"

"The little troublemaker will regret spying on us, I can tell you that much!"

Dexter didn't like the sound of that at all. He closed the closet door quietly behind him and dove headfirst into the mountain. He clawed his way through the pile of lost and forgotten items.

2 DIRECTION
JUSTIN BEAVER
GORGE MICHAEL
NO NUKES!
SMOOCH
BUTTLES!

Down and down he burrowed. He thought the mountain might go on forever, when suddenly it seemed to open up and he found himself in an open cavelike space.

When he heard the sound of the closet door opening and the muffled voices of Mr. McFur and the stranger, he froze.

"Well, he obviously isn't in here."

"Perhaps not . . . AHA!"

"You see him?"

"No. But I had an ALF shirt just like this. I still mourn the cancellation of that TV show. Keepsies!"

Dexter heard the door close, and he breathed a deep sigh of relief. But just to be on the safe side, he decided he would wait a while before trying to head home.

While he waited, he took a good look at the lost junk around him. It was mostly just a bunch of old toys and a skateboard that had seen better days. He picked up the board. It was pretty old—chipped and covered in scratches—but still . . . he'd always wanted a skateboard. *No one would call me boring if I could ride a skateboard like Toby Falcon*, he thought.

But taking the skateboard from the pile would be stealing. And Dexter wasn't a thief. He put the board down with a sigh. "Well, I hope you find your owner someday."

By now, he figured McFur and the stranger would be long gone. Quietly, Dexter crept out of the office. He didn't see anyone in the hallway. No one jumped out at him unexpectedly as he made his way to the school's front doors. But he did spot something glittering and metallic in the middle of the hallway and picked it up. It was a tin of mustache wax. None of the kids at Kirby Richards Elementary had a mustache. None of the teachers did either. Well, except Mr. McFur. But he'd never seen his teacher use wax before. Dexter put it in his pocket and headed home.

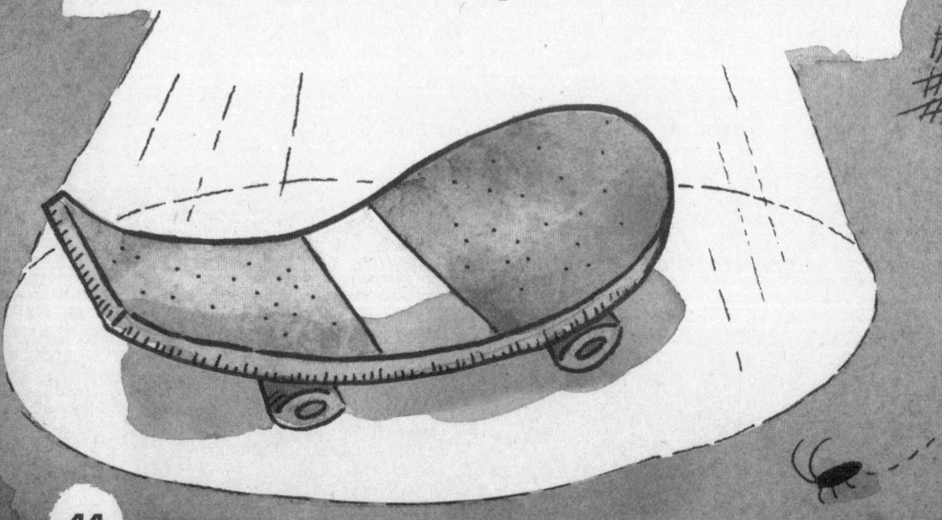

EXIT
As he left, Dexter didn't realize that something was watching him from the shadows . . .

CHAPTER 4

Gamma Broccoli and Giant Rats!

The next day, Dexter shot into Mr. McFur's classroom (late again!) just as a man from Animal Control grabbed the last of the full rat cages from Mr. McFur. The whole class was in tears. Principal Pickles was, too. Pretty perched on Mr. McFur's shoulder, her whiskers trembling in fear.

"Well," the man said gruffly, "that's all of the vermin, except one." He held out his hand expectantly toward Mr. McFur.

The man meant Pretty. Everyone gasped—well, everyone except for the mean Animal Control guy. Then a strange smile crept over Mr. McFur's face as he removed a single stalk of broccoli from his pocket.

"You won't take away my babies," he declared. "Not when you all witness what Rat Gas Power™ can do." He put Pretty on the desk and fed her a bit of the strange, glowing broccoli. Pretty let out a small toot, but nothing much happened.

The man from Animal Control laughed cruelly and snatched Pretty from the desk. "Dunderdolt Plotz always gets his rat!"

But while he was speaking, Pretty began to glow strangely. And then she started to grow.

And **GROW**.

AND GROW SOME MORE.

Soon Pretty was the size of an elephant. One who was really, really hungry.

Some children hid under desks. Others ran screaming from the room. Millicent tried to climb into one of the empty cages to disguise herself as one of Pretty's little friends.

But the rat's giant, bulging eyes fell upon Principal Pickles. Pretty licked her lips and opened her mouth wide.

MMPH!

BOINK!
Throw!

"Oh dear, oh dear, oh dear . . ." Principal Pickles whimpered.

Pretty was about to swallow Principal Pickles whole when suddenly a stapler bounced off the rat monster's nose. Pretty turned, eyes glowing with with rage, and saw Dexter standing there with another stapler in hand.

"Leave her alone!" Dexter yelled. And then he threw the second stapler at Pretty. It gave her a whack on the head that was more annoying to the monster than painful. The rat let loose a monstrous roar, then turned and started running toward him.

While Dexter's actions were brave, they were also totally dumb. He'd saved Principal Pickles from certain digestion, but now it looked like he was going to be lunch for a giant mutated rat!

Mr. McFur grabbed Pretty's ginormous tail and tried to slow her down. Through gritted teeth he cried,

And run Dexter did. He may have been boring, he may have been bland, but the one thing Dexter had going for him was speed. He tore out of the room, and sprinted down the corridor.

But then the tail slipped through McFur's hands, and the mutant rat crashed through the door.

Dexter had to find a phone . . . fast! He would call his parents. No, wait, the police. No, even better, the Marines!!!

He knew the rat was closing on him. He could practically feel the creature's hot breath on his neck. *At least my death won't be boring!* he thought.

Halfway down the hall, Dexter spied something he couldn't quite believe.

A skateboard sat in the middle of the hallway. And it wasn't just any skateboard—it was the one that he had discovered in the office closet last night! *What's it doing here?* he wondered.

But however it had gotten there, he was glad to see it. He jumped on the board and kicked as hard as he could, escaping Pretty's grasp just as she was about to slash Dexter with her gigantic claws.

Dexter flew down the hallway atop the skateboard. He rolled through doorways and swerved at lightning speed, and suddenly found himself in the school stairwell.

Instead of tumbling down the stairs, Dexter and the board leapt onto the railing. As they slid down it, the board began to hum with energy. It let loose a roar like a small airplane taking off, and then shot forward like a rocket.

Dexter dropped onto his stomach and clung tightly to the board, screaming his head off the whole time. "What are you doing? We're never going to make it. Tell my mom I love her and I'm sorry I never pick up my dirty socks!" he yelled to no one in particular.

The skateboard leapt high into the air, crashed through the classroom ceiling, and then propelled itself out into the open air, leaving the school and certain doom behind!

Dexter flew high above the school. He could see all the evacuated students and teachers, small like ants on the ground below. Fire trucks and police cars were just now arriving on the scene.

As they passed basketball courts and dry cleaning shops, Dexter noticed that the skateboard was headed somewhere oddly familiar. It seemed as though the board was headed for the subway!

As if the skateboard could read Dexter's mind, it took a sudden nosedive into the entrance of the subway station.

Dexter began to panic, and it only got worse when he heard a familiar rumble and an even more familiar blaring horn.

"Please don't go on the tracks," Dexter pleaded. "Please, please, **PLEASE** don't go on the tracks!" The board zipped down the stairs and onto the platform, narrowly avoiding the subway train that was just then pulling into the station. "Whew!" sighed Dexter. "That was a close one."

START!
SKATE
Secret Passage
F
Al Capone's other Vault
Lost Sock Nest

But before he could catch his breath, the board rushed down the platform and flew straight at the Skate Spy movie poster Dexter had noticed the day before.

They were going to hit the wall. Dexter was about to become another stain on the concrete. But just in the nick of time, the movie poster slid away, revealing a black hole behind it. Seconds later, Dexter and the crazy flying skateboard tumbled into the darkness beyond!

CHAPTER 5

Spymasters and Old Grudges!

One minute Dexter was zooming through the air, and the next the board had stopped abruptly and Dexter tumbled off. He rolled over in a couple of awkward somersaults and landed on his back with a loud "**Oof!**"

He sat up shakily and looked around the cavernous space. It was full of strange, futuristic computer equipment that blinked and beeped and belched.

1 Up!
BREAKING NEWS! ANIMAL ON THE LOOSE!
Kirby Richards
25¢
Beep!
PNN
K
PIZZA!

He had just enough time to wonder where he was before he heard a grumbling voice coming from a large chair at the far end of the cavern. "I thought I told you to never show your ugly, old, busted face in these parts again!"

Dexter was very confused. He wasn't ugly. Was he? He'd never thought so. And he was sure he'd never been through the wall of a subway platform before.

"I thought I told you to stay out of my secret headquarters!" The voice in the chair swiveled around quickly.

Sitting in it was the eye-patched subway musician. She rose and stomped over to the old skateboard.

Is she talking to a skateboard? wondered Dexter. *She must be crazy. And I thought the giant rat was scary!*

But then things got really weird. The skateboard stood up on its rear wheels and started yelling back. Instead of shouting in a normal human voice, it bellowed things like "Bzzblik!" and "Bleep!" But all the same, it was clearly yelling at the girl with the eye patch.

They both fell silent, facing each other. The musician (who, by the way, was so NOT a musician—Dexter could have told you that chapters ago) crossed her arms, tapped one combat-booted foot, and scowled angrily at the skateboard.

The skateboard looked just as angry. Dexter couldn't have said exactly how, as it was a skateboard. It just did.

Dexter cleared his throat. "Excuse me, but, um, where am I?" he asked timidly.

The eye patch turned on him. "You are an unauthorized intruder in the headquarters of the Super-Secret Spy Kids, Local Girder City Chapter. And I'm Big K. The Big Kid in Charge. Like it or leave it."

Dexter pointed at the skateboard. "And that flying skateboard is . . . ?"

"A traitor." She scowled.

The skateboard flew into another flurry of frazzled bleeps and static blips in response.

"They were a great team, secretly toppling evil regimes, spoiling evil plots, defeating bad guys left and right.

"But they couldn't stay out of the limelight. They started entering skating competitions . . . and winning. Eventually, Hollywood called. Toby couldn't say no to fame and fortune. He forgot the very first rule of the Super-Secret Spy Kids . . .

STAY SECRET!

"Now I've lost my best spy just when I need him most. This has to be the work of the stolen gamma broccoli!"

Dexter was shocked. "You know about the broccoli?"

SUPER-SECRET KID FILE

AGENT B.O.A.R.D.

(Battery Operated Artificial Reasoning Device)

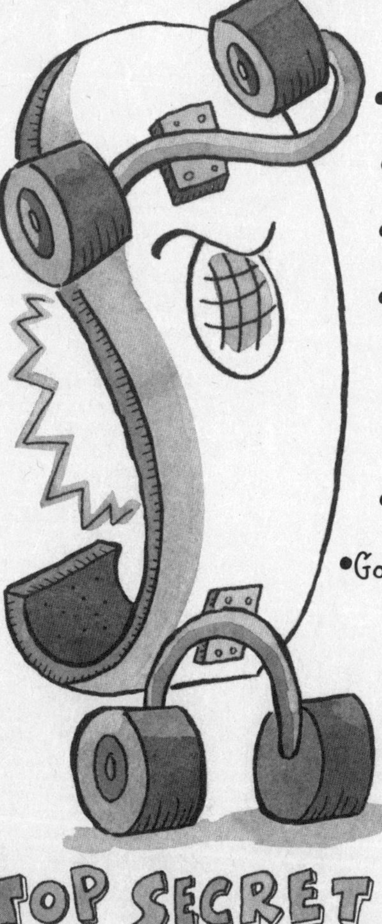

- Cost over $1,000,000!
- Wheel extenders!
- Super computer brain!
- Really good chef!
- Night vision!
- Super loyal!
- Epic rail slides!
- Good with the ladies!
- Cardsharp!
- Super fast!
- All the stuff!

TOP SECRET INFO, YO!

Big K raised an eyebrow. "I've been tracking it for days. More importantly, how do you know about the broccoli?"

"I saw some man give it to my teacher, Mr. McFur." Dexter looked miserable. "Mr. McFur isn't a bad person. He just didn't want his rats taken away. This is all my fault!"

Big K put a hand on his shoulder. "Pfft. You were gathering intel, and trying to use it wisely. Kid, that's exactly what I would have done."

"But now Pretty is going to eat Principal Pickles and Mr. McFur is going to go to jail!"

Big K thought for a moment. "Maybe not. There might be a way we can save both Mr. McFur and Principal Pickles."

"But how?" asked Dexter.

Big K answered gruffly, "Follow me."

CHAPTER 6

The Next Super-Secret Spy Kid!

Big K, Dexter, and a rather sad-looking B.O.A.R.D. stopped in front of a wall of lockers. She opened the door to #8. "This was Toby's locker. It contains all his old equipment. He left it behind when he quit."

Big K clenched her fists. "Toby's assignment was simple. Be a kid. Be a normal schoolkid, until danger threatened. And then be a spy fighting for truth and justice!"

Dexter laughed. “You sound like a superhero.”

She handed him Toby’s helmet. “Maybe because the world needs superheroes. Superheroes who are willing to fight for what’s right.”

BAD SPY!
GOOD SPY!
Perfect hair!
Extra bendy eyebrow
Chiseled jaw
Teeth too shiny
Muscley
Tailored tuxedo
Keys to crazy-awesome sports car
Fancy shoes
Nervous at parties
Favorite hat
Clip-on tie
Collects pens
Bus pass
Pants not tailored
Supported loafers

Dexter took the helmet. "Wait a minute. Me? You want me to become the next Super-Secret Spy Kid? But I'm so . . . so . . . **BORING**!"

"That's what makes you perfect. You're a regular kid. Toby was not. He was a star. He wanted to be famous. I see that now. Superstars make for lousy spies. The best spies are invisible. They're your next-door neighbor or the harmless old man down the street. Successful spies look boring on the outside, but are heroes on the inside. You're the only one in your class who recognized the danger Mr. McFur was in. You're the only one who tried to help him. You don't know it, but you're much, much more than an average third grader, Dexter Drabner. Your Mr. McFur has only one chance to avoid spending the rest of his days behind bars. And that's you. If you think you're up to it."

"If you're in, take that elevator down to the training floor. I'll give you a minute to think about it." Big K started to walk away, but stopped at the door. "Either way, that was a pretty great speech I got to make just then. And spymasters love a good speech!"

The elevator doors closed behind her.

Dexter looked at the helmet that would hide his identity, the super-high-tech gear in the locker, and then at the skateboard. He took a deep breath. "What have I gotten myself into?" he asked. B.O.A.R.D. looked up at him, improbably wagging its tail.

When the elevator doors opened, Big K was looking at some top secret files that were so incredibly secret you aren't allowed to see them. Behind her a voice said, "Dex Drabner, new (but not improved) Super-Secret Spy Kid reporting for duty."

Big K nodded. "Good," she said. "Now let's get you ready for your first mission . . ."

TOP SECRET
TRAINING
ROOM

SKATE TRAINING
COMBAT TRAINING
Haiya!
BLOCKED!

STEALTH TRAINING
Where is he?
Chew!
Chew!
PB+J!
Bologna!
LUNCH

After Dex's training session, Big K handed him a giant pill that was almost as big as his head.

"What's Gas-B-Gone?" Dex asked, looking a bit skeptical.

"It's a little something to help you put things straight. From what I've observed, that rat has the worst gas in the history of the world—gamma gas. That's what's blown her up. We need to deflate her. Trust me. This will do the trick."

"Great. So we'll just fly in . . ."

"Bleep! Bloop. Woo." B.O.A.R.D. sounded sad.

Big K frowned. "He says that he's out of rocket booster fuel. It's what lets him fly. But he only has so much, and he used it up saving your pathetic patootie."

Dex patted the skateboard and smiled. "Well, thanks for that, pal. No worries, we'll do the rest of this old school."

Twenty minutes later, Dex and B.O.A.R.D. were huddled behind a bush on the edge of the school grounds.

The first trick, Dex knew, was coming up with a plan to sneak back into the building. But with all the police officers, firemen, reporters, teachers, and concerned parents surrounding it, Dex couldn't see a way to slip in unnoticed. He needed to do this ninja-style!

"Bzzz bzzzt," the skateboard whispered, and somehow Dex understood. It sounded like it had said, "Let's create a diversion."

"That's a great idea, B.O.A.R.D. But how?"

The board rolled toward a white van parked beside a television news truck.

The side of the van read "Animal Control." In front of it stood a familiar, unwelcome character. Animal Control Officer Dunderdolt Plotz was being interviewed by a television reporter.

B.O.A.R.D. gestured with his wheel at the back door of the van. Now Dex got it! The rats that Plotz had taken from the classroom were probably still inside.

"All right, B.O.A.R.D., time for stealth mode." Dexter lay down on B.O.A.R.D. and the two of them rolled under the van. The door was unlocked, but the rat cages inside all had big padlocks on them.

"Blip!" A small metallic arm extended from one of B.O.A.R.D.'s front wheels. And at the end of the arm was a skeleton key . . .

Officer Dunderdolt Plotz was having a good day. A success of this size could win him a promotion, maybe even help him become Director of Animal Control. And a flattering interview wouldn't hurt his chances.

"You see, miss, rats have been a problem since the beginning of time."

KIRBY RICHARDS ELEMENTARY
ANIMAL CONTROL

Action News reporter Missy Smiley corrected him. "I'm pretty sure rats weren't around at the beginning of time."

Suddenly a small gray face poked its head out of her big television hairdo. Then three more small rodent heads popped out.

Dunderdolt pointed. "Um, miss, I think you have something in your hair."

"Oh, thank you." She reached up, pulled out a rat, looked at it for a moment, and then screamed louder than a fire alarm.

Suddenly rats were everywhere. They were on teachers and students, on cameras and firemen's hats and police cars. Everyone was shouting and shaking the rodents off. If Dexter hadn't known better, he'd have said it looked like a dance party.

ANIMAL
CONTROL

Woo!
Woo!
POLICE
GIRDER CITY
POPO1
FIRE

"Eww! Rats!" yelled a fireman. "It's a plaque! A plaque!"

"Plaque is tooth decay, dear," one of the fourth grade teachers corrected him. "This is a *plague*, with a *g*."

The diversion had worked perfectly. While everyone's attention was on the rats, Dex and B.O.A.R.D. skated quickly through the police barricade and into the school.

CHAPTER 7

Pep Talks and Daring Rescues!

The abandoned school was eerily quiet. Dexter searched the halls, wondering where Pretty might be. The most obvious place to search for the rat was Mr. McFur's classroom. But all he found there was Mr. McFur, looking more dejected than ever.

"Dexter?" he asked. "You have to get out of here. Pretty has already taken Principal Pickles. I don't want her to get you, too."

"Mr. McFur, we have to do something!"

Mr. McFur let out a sad chuckle. "Sure, a failure of a science teacher and a third grader with a skateboard are going to defeat Ratzilla."

"Trust me, sir, this isn't your average, everyday skateboard," said Dexter. "Do you know where they are?"

Mr. McFur nodded sadly. "My sweet petunia has made a nest in the auditorium." He shook his head. "Even if you find them, what good will it do?"

Dex held up the giant Gas-B-Gone pill. "If we can get Pretty to swallow this, we may be able to save Principal Pickles."

McFur wiped his snotty nose on his shirtsleeve. "But how? My Rat Mind Molder™ doesn't work on Pretty's mutated brain!" He slumped down and put his head in his hands. "It's hopeless. I'm just a big loser."

"Listen, Mr. McFur," Dex said. "When I woke up this morning, I thought I was no one special, just boring old Dexter Drabner. And now I'm about to use a flying robotic skateboard to rescue our principal from a giant mutated rat. You're no more hopeless than I was boring. You just have to have a little faith in yourself. I do."

Dex gave his teacher a pat on the back. Then he hopped on B.O.A.R.D. and skated off.

Mr. McFur watched him go. *If Dex gets out of this mess alive*, thought McFur, *I'll give him extra credit for this. Definitely.*

GAS-B-GONE

The auditorium was dark except for a few footlights on the stage pointed directly at Pretty, who lay sprawled in front of a fake skyscraper. The school musical that year was going to be *43rd Street* and the set looked like the Girder City skyline.

Dex rolled silently down a carpeted aisle toward the stage. He could see a worried Principal Pickles poking out from beneath one of the rat's giant paws. Pretty was out cold, her loud snores echoing through the auditorium.

He crept up onto the stage. Dex winced at every creak of the old wooden floorboards. When he finally reached Principal Pickles, Dex held his finger to his lips, the universal symbol for "Be really, **REALLY** quiet, or this giant rat might wake up and eat both of us!"

He grabbed Principal Pickles's hands and started to pull with all his might. Little by little, he worked her free.

Almost there! Dex thought. Just a couple more inches and . . .

Then Dex rolled right over Pretty's pink, snakelike tail.

Oops.

SMACK

Pretty's eyes snapped open. She reared up on her hind legs, snatching Principal Pickles in one paw like a favorite doll. *Holy guacamole!* Dexter thought, just before the rat swatted him like a fly.

Pretty had woken up grumpy with hunger, and now her tail smarted. She looked ready to eat the little boy who'd done it, then pick her teeth with Principal Pickles afterward.

It sure looked like the end of the road for Dex Drabner, Super-Secret Spy Kid!

CHAPTER 8

Rise of the BROdent!

Just as the giant rodent was about to drop Dex into her mouth, she was besieged by an army of tiny rats! Dozens and dozens of them zipped around her on skateboards, distracting her. She roared in frustration as they ollied off of her nose, used her tail to catch serious air, and flashed by her at lightning speeds.

A voice rang out through the darkened auditorium. "Onward, my dear skate rats! Rescue the boy! Save the principal!" A large figure stepped out of the shadows and into the light.

"Mr . . . Mr. McFur?" Principal Pickles asked.

"You once knew me as Mr. McFur, Principal Pickles, but now you may call me . . . the BROdent! Bro to rodents everywhere. And thanks to some wise words from that boy right there, I'm here to fix the mess I made!"

"Oh my!" said Principal Pickles.

Pretty roared in frustration as the gnatlike skate rats surrounded her. She swatted at them, but when that didn't stop them, she tried to escape them by climbing the Girder City Skyscraper.

The BROdent leapt up onto the stage and ran over to Dex.

"Dexter!" he cried. "Are you all right?"

Dex took in Mr. McFur's outlandish getup. "Where did you get that superhero outfit?"

"Oh, it's just something I keep around for parties." The BROdent knocked on his metallic helmet. "And this is a modified version of my Rat Mind Molder, still TM."

He glanced up at Pretty, who clung tightly to the very top of the tower . . . and to Principal Pickles. "How are we going to get them down?"

Dex pointed to his skateboard. "I could fly up there with this little guy, but he's out of rocket booster fuel."

"Bloo," B.O.A.R.D. sadly agreed.

"Hmm," said Mr. McFur, "let me take a look."

The BROdent tinkered a bit with the skateboard and then smiled. “I’ve connected the board’s booster jets to its power core. It’ll give you one more giant jump, but that will be it.” He looked at Dex. “This is extraordinarily dangerous. Are you sure you want to try it?”

SCOON!

Dex looked at B.O.A.R.D. and the skateboard looked at Dex. They both nodded.

"We've only got one shot at this," said Dex as he hefted the giant Gas-B-Gone pill. "Let's do it."

He climbed on B.O.A.R.D. and kicked off. The two shot up toward the rat like a Fourth of July firecracker.

CHARD!
GAS-B-GONE

Dex flew straight at Pretty's open, snarling mouth with the force of a cannonball. He flung the Gas-B-Gone pill down Pretty's throat and tried to make a U-turn. But at that very moment, B.O.A.R.D. used up the last of its power, and turned off like a light.

10!
THROW!
GASB-GONE
GASB-GONE

Oh, sherbet, Dex thought, as Pretty closed her mouth. The rat felt something fly down her throat. It tickled like crazy. And it tasted rather skateboardy.

Gulp! She swallowed Dex and the skateboard whole.

Pretty burped.

She didn't feel so hot. Frankly, she hadn't felt very well since she had eaten that broccoli her beloved master had fed her earlier in the day. She climbed down from the tower, stumbled off the stage, and clomped down the hall to the one place in the school that felt like home: Mr. McFur's classroom.

She shouldn't have eaten whatever it was that had zipped into her mouth. Now her tummy hurt.

When Pretty finally reached the classroom, her stomachache had become too much for her. She dropped Principal Pickles and began to heave into the nearest desk.

Out of Pretty's mouth gushed buckets of disgusting slime, one full-size boy, one robotic skateboard, and some glowing bits of radioactive broccoli.

Pop!
Pop!

The giant rat slumped to the floor. And then, finally, Pretty began to fart. With each toxic rumble, she felt a little better. And with each toot of gas, the lights in the classroom got brighter and brighter, until the bulbs exploded from the surge.

Principal Pickles gasped. “Mr. McFur was right all along,” she cried. “Rat farts actually do create electric power!”

Soon Pretty started to feel a little . . . littler.

Gas began to whistle out of her with such force that the rat started to fly around the room like a popped helium balloon.

CHAPTER 9

The End

At last Pretty floated to the ground, utterly deflated. She came to land safely on Mr. McFur's desk.

The BROdent rushed into the classroom. "Thank goodness you're all right!" He ran past Principal Pickles and Dex to poor, exhausted Pretty and covered her with kisses.

When he was sure Pretty was okay, he turned to Dex. "Thank you for your help, D—"

Dex shook his head furiously. He didn't want Principal Pickles to know his secret identity.

Mr. McFur winked. "I mean, thank you for your help, Super-Secret Spy Kid."

Principal Pickles rushed up to Mr. McFur. "You were right!" she cried. "Pretty blew out every light bulb with her megafarts! You're going to change the world!"

"No he won't!" a voice from above called.

Dex looked up. Swinging down a zip line through the classroom ceiling was Big K. He could hear the sound of a helicopter in the distance.

Big K landed with a thud and turned to the BROdent. "The world just isn't ready for this sort of power. If it falls into the wrong hands it could be disastrous. For your protection, I've been ordered to take you and your rat fart technology into custody. And this as well!" She stooped and picked up a bit of the half-digested glowing gamma broccoli.

"Mr. McFur, I have a proposition for you," Big K continued. "Why don't you come work for me? My last scientist/inventor disappeared on me, and a spymaster without a good scientist/inventor is almost as useless as a spymaster without an eye patch and a closet full of black outfits. Take my hand, McFur. You'll be happier in the private sector. Trust me."

Big K had collected all the tiny bits of radioactive broccoli, and put them safely in a glass vial. She pulled an ID card out of her pocket and handed it to Dex. "Nice work. You saved the school and retrieved the stolen broccoli. Consider your first mission a success. And welcome to the Super-Secret Spy Kids, Agent SK8!"

Then, against all odds, Big K actually smiled!

The BROdent turned to Dex. "See you around, Agent SK8. And thank you for helping me do the right thing!"

"But what about B.O.A.R.D.?" Dex cried. His partner had heroically sacrificed himself to save them all. It broke Dexter's heart to look at the lifeless skateboard.

Big K opened a compartment in the rear truck of the skateboard.

"No worries, kid. B.O.A.R.D.'s batteries may be kaput right now, but you can recharge them. You just need to plug him in overnight. He should be good as new by the morning. But it's one of those three-plug thingamajigs that you can never find when you need one. It can be a real pain!"

Dex suddenly remembered something. He reached into his pocket and handed Mr. McFur the tin of mustache wax he had found in the hallway.

"Here, Mr. McFur. I think you dropped this."

Mr. McFur took one look and handed it back to Dex. "That's not mine. I don't use mustache wax."

"But if it's not yours, then whose is it?" Suddenly, Dex realized that this tin might be a clue to the identity of the stranger who'd talked Mr. McFur into this whole mess!

Big K grabbed the BROdent's hand, then tugged hard on the rope. Instantly the two were pulled up through the skylight.

Principal Pickles surveyed the damage around her. Then she turned to Dex. "You look familiar, Agent SK8. Very, very familiar." She leaned in closely. "Why don't you take off those goggles so I can get a good look at your face, hmm?"

Uh-oh, Dexter thought. He couldn't reveal who he was, or Principal Pickles would tell his parents, and his new job as a superspy would be over after just one mission. Dex had to act fast! "Shouldn't you let someone know that the school's safe?" he asked.

Principal Pickles practically jumped into the air. "Goodness me! You're right. I should go tell the authorities! You stay right here. I'm going to be curious to see the boy behind that mask!" she called as she hurried off.

Dex ran to his locker and shoved B.O.A.R.D. and his spy gear inside. He'd have to recharge his friend later when he got home. He barely had time to shut the door before Millicent strolled around the corner with her friends. "**HEY, LOOK! IT'S SNOOZYPANTS! WHERE YA BEEN, WONDERBREAD? YOU MISSED ALL THE ACTION.**"

"Action? What action? I've been reading in the library . . ."

Millicent broke out into fits of laughter. "**ONLY BLAND, BORING DEXTER DRABNER WOULD MISS THE COOLEST THING TO HAPPEN IN KIRBY RICHARDS ELEMENTARY EVER! HAR HAR!**"

As Millicent and her friends strutted past him, Millicent couldn't resist elbowing Dex in the ribs.

But Dex just smiled. "Yep, that's me. Dexter Drabner, the most boring boy in school."

CHAPTER 10

Okay. This Is the Actual End. For Real. Because Aren't You Curious about What Happens to Everyone? I Know I Am!

DEXTER DRABNER

[AKA Super-Secret Spy Kid, Agent SK8]

Dex carried on in his role as Agent SK8. He has to hide his new job from his parents, but they're happy he's "making friends" and "getting some fresh air."

B.O.A.R.D.

B.O.A.R.D. was recharged and is adjusting to artificial life with his new partner. Dex's parents aren't sure where the skateboard came from, but are thrilled that Dexter has a hobby.

BIG K

[Real Identity CLASSIFIED]

Big K still heads the Super-Secret Spy Kids, Local Girder City Chapter. And if you have a problem with that, **TOUGH**.

MR. MCFUR

[AKA The BROdent]

Mr. McFur is now the new Chief Scientist/ Inventor at the Local Girder City Chapter. He has retired his BROdent persona, except for the occasional party and bar mitzvah.

PRINCIPAL PICKLES

Principal Pickles continues in her role as principal of Kirby Richards Elementary. She has developed a real phobia about rats and is still wondering who that masked kid was.

DUNDERDOLT PLOTZ

Officer Dunderdolt Plotz was let go from his position at Animal Control. Plotz was last seen vowing to "chase that giant mutant rat to the ends of the earth, and **BEYOND!**"

MILLICENT M.

Millicent was proud of herself for getting McFur fired—until she met the new science teacher. Now the class goes on community-service field trips and keeps cute, fluffy white bunny rabbits as pets.

THE STRANGER

[Real Identity UNKNOWN]

So who was that stranger who gave Mr. McFur the gamma broccoli? And WHY? You'll have to wait for the next book to find that out. **NOT COOL**.

Don't miss Dex's next thrilling mission!

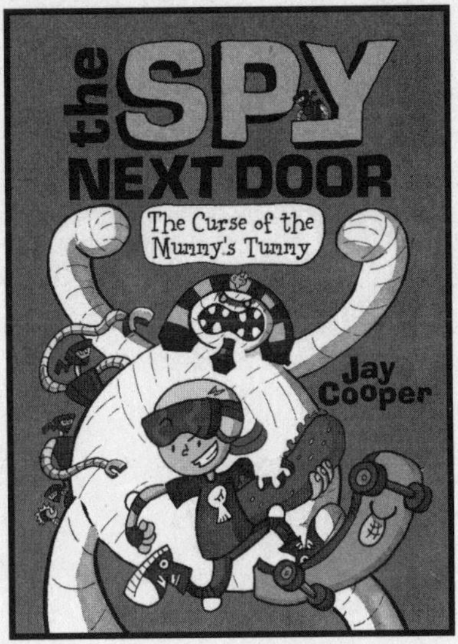

An Egyptian treasure that can raise the dead is missing from the museum! And with an army of robot ninjas, a mustachioed mystery man, and a sneaky new classmate lurking around every corner, it's up to Dex to find it first and save the world from a monstrous mummy's ancient curse . . .

HEY!
Let's get something straight! In this book, Dex does some pretty crazy stunts on his skateboard.
But he's had special training. And he's a cartoon character!!!
YOU are not a cartoon character. So don't try any of these stunts, even if your skateboard is a million-dollar-government-created robot!!!

NO!
YES!
BUT...
Even though Dex isn't a real person, he still doesn't shred without wearing his SAFETY GEAR!
Yup, I drew those.
SAFETY GEAR
•Helmet
•Elbow Pads
•Knee Pads
•Wrist Guards